HORIZONS

Reading to Learn

Fast Track C–D
Workbook 2

Siegfried Engelmann

Susan Hanner

SRA
McGraw-Hill

Columbus, Ohio

A Division of The McGraw-Hill Companies

Illustration Credits

Rick Cooley, Simon Galkin, Heidi King, Den Schofield, Jessica Stanley.

SRA/McGraw-Hill

A Division of The McGraw·Hill Companies

Send all inquiries to:
SRA/McGraw-Hill
8787 Orion Place
Columbus, OH 43240-4027

ISBN 0-02-674219-5

7 8 9 10 POH 06 05 04 03

A

1. Palm trees cannot live in places that get ▬▬.

    • wet   • cold   • moist

2. What are the branches of palm trees called?

    • fans   • fonds   • fronds

B Story Items

3. **Name 2 ways that the stream water was different from the ocean water.**

   The water in the stream was _____ and

   _____.

4. A strange sound woke Linda in the morning. What was making that strange sound?

    • sailors   • birds   • waves

5. Whose footprints did Linda and Kathy find on the beach?

   _____

6. Linda said, "We have been walking in a circle. That means we're ▬▬."

    • in a forest   • near Japan   • on an island

7. Did Linda and Kathy see anyone else when they were

   walking? _____

The map shows the island that Linda and Kathy were on.

8. Write **north, south, east,** and **west** in the right boxes.

9. **Draw a line** from the crate to show where Linda and Kathy walked.

10. **Make an X** to show where Linda was when she saw footprints.

11. **Make a Y** to show where they landed on the island.

12. **Make an S** to show where the stream is.

13. **Circle** the grove where they found bananas.

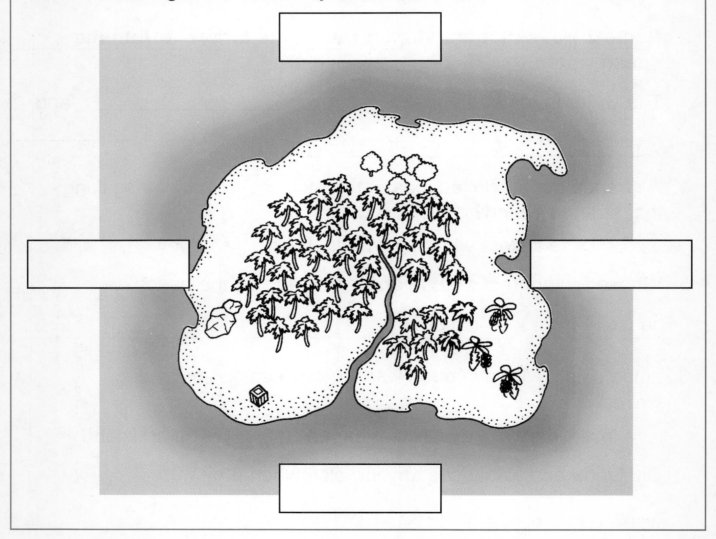

GO TO PART D IN YOUR TEXTBOOK.

A Story Items

1. What was wrong with the first coconuts that the girls found?

    • They were too high in the trees.

    • They were not ripe.

    • They were rotten.

2. When Kathy shook the coconut, it sounded like a bottle that had water in it. What made the sound like water?

    _____

3. What did Linda and Kathy use to open the coconut?

    _____

4. Why did the girls want to make the monkeys mad?

    • so they would go away

    • so they would make noise

    • so they would throw coconuts

The picture shows a coconut.

5. Make an **X** on the part that the girls ate.

6. Make a **Y** on the part that the girls drank.

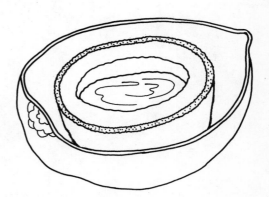

Review Items

The map shows the island that Linda and Kathy were on.

7. Write **north, south, east,** and **west** in the right boxes.

8. **Draw a line** from the crate to show where Linda and Kathy walked.

9. **Make an A** to show where Linda was when she saw footprints.

10. **Make a B** to show where they landed on the island.

11. **Make a C** to show where the stream is.

12. **Circle** the grove where they found bananas.

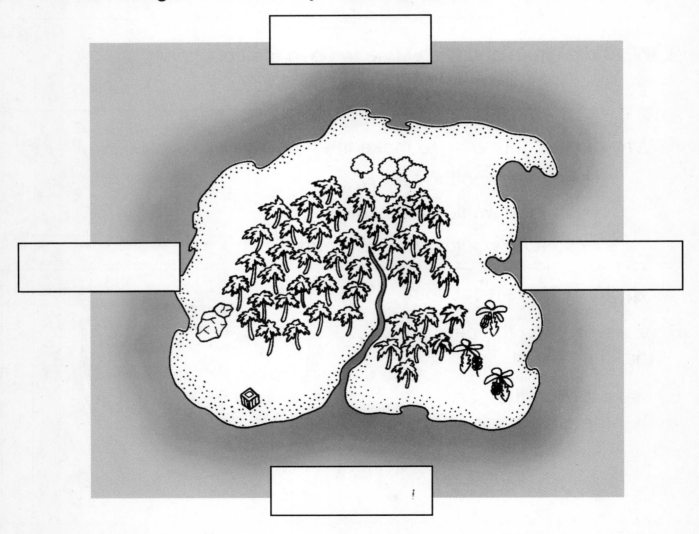

GO TO PART D IN YOUR TEXTBOOK.

A

1. All machines make it easier for someone to _____.

2. You would have the most power if you pushed against one of the handles. Which handle is that? _____

3. Which handle would give you the least amount of power?

_____

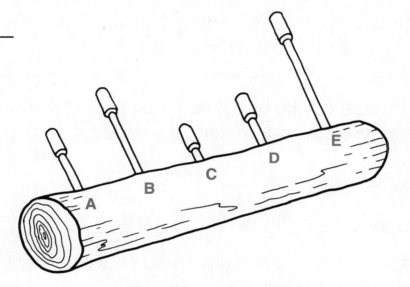

B **Story Items**

4. What were the only things Linda and Kathy ate for two days?

- carrots   • coconuts   • corn
- fronds   • bananas   • cabbage

5. Why did Linda and Kathy want to catch some fish?

     • They were tired.

     • They wanted to eat something new.

     • They could not open the coconuts.

6. What did they use for fish hooks? _____

7. What did they use for a fishing line? _____

8. Were there many fish in the water? _____

9. Did Linda and Kathy catch many fish with their hooks and

    lines? _____

10. The girls made hooks and lines to catch fish. Then they
    made something else to catch fish. What else did they

    make? _____

11. What did they make it out of? _____

12. What happened when the girls tried to pull the net out of the
    water?

     • The fish jumped out of the water.

     • The fish pulled the girls into the water.

     • The crate fell in the water.

GO TO PART D IN YOUR TEXTBOOK.

A Story Items

1. Linda and Kathy built something to help them ▮▮▮.
    - pull the nails from the crate
    - pull the net from the ocean
    - pull Kathy's teeth

2. What did the girls find floating in the water?
    - a ship
    - a first aid kit
    - boards

3. The white box probably came from ▮▮▮.
    - their ship
    - their crate
    - Italy

4. What was the most important thing inside the box?
    - candy
    - food
    - matches

5. Why didn't the girls test them right away?
    - They would need them later.
    - They didn't know how.
    - They were tired.

6. The girls made a ▮▮▮.
    - building
    - machine
    - motor

7. What did the girls use for a handle?
    - a board
    - a log
    - a vine

8. The girls hammered the handle to the end of ████.

    • a shoe   • a log   • a crate

9. The girls got nails from ████.

    • a shoe   • a log   • a crate

10. They tied one end of the vine to the log and the other end of the vine to the ████.

    • beach   • crate   • net

11. When the fish were in the net, the girls ████.

    • turned the handle   • ran into the water

           • climbed a tree

12. The arrow by the handle shows which way it turns. Make an arrow on the log to show which way it turns.

13. Make an arrow by the vine to show which way it moves.

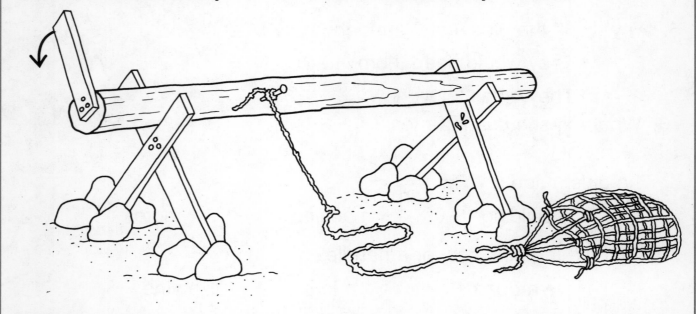

GO TO PART C IN YOUR TEXTBOOK.

A

1. What is it called when the sun goes down?

  • sunrise   • sunset

2. What is it called when the sun comes up?

  • sunrise   • sunset

B **Story Items**

3. What did Kathy have to do to the outside of the fish?

  • remove fins   • remove scales   • remove shells

4. What did she use for a tool?

  • a fin   • a scale   • a shell

5. What was Linda's job when the girls cleaned the fish?

  • removing the scales   • removing the insides

  • removing the fins

6. What did she use for a tool?

  • a belt buckle   • a nail   • a rock

7. Linda made her tool sharp by ▇▇▇▇.

  • rubbing it against a rock   • putting it in the fire

  • making it red hot

8. Name 2 things the girls ate for dinner.

  1 _____

  2 _____

9. Linda and Kathy drank fresh water with their dinner.

   Where did they get the fresh water? _____

10. **Underline** 4 things that the girls used to make their simple machine.

   - vines
   - boards
   - turtle shell

   - nails
   - rope
   - matches

   - coconuts
   - a tree trunk

Review Items

11. The arrow by the handle shows which way it turns. Make an arrow on the log to show which way it moves.

12. Make an arrow by the vine to show which way it moves.

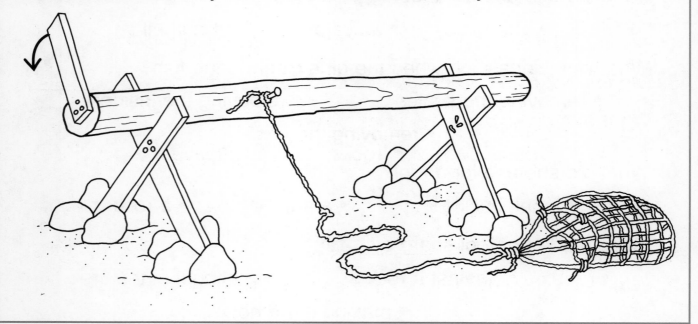

GO TO PART D IN YOUR TEXTBOOK.

A

1. The temperature inside your body is about _____ degrees.

2. Most fevers don't go over _____ degrees.

3. When people have very high fevers, they may see and hear things that are not _____.

B   **Story Items**

4. How long had Linda and Kathy been on the island when they saw the airplane?

   • 15 days   • 3 weeks   • 12 days

5. Did the people in the plane see Linda and Kathy? _____

6. What did the girls use to make a signal for planes?

   • paint   • rocks   • leaves

7. What word did they spell? _____

8. The word was over _____ feet long.

9. What kind of signal did the girls have ready for ships?

   • rocks   • fog   • smoke

10. What would make the fire smoke?

   • sticks   • green leaves   • bananas

11. How did Linda know that Kathy had a fever?

  • Linda felt her forehead.

  • Linda took her temperature.

  • Linda felt her feet.

12. Linda thought that Kathy's temperature was over

  _____ degrees.

Review Items

13. The United States is a _____.

  • city   • state   • country

14. Japan is a _____.

15. The United States is made up of fifty _____.

GO TO PART D IN YOUR TEXTBOOK.

A

1. Put a **T** on each tugboat.

2. Put a **D** on each dock.

3. Put an **S** on each ship.

B **Story Items**

4. How long had Linda and Kathy been on the island when they saw the airplane?

     • 15 days   • 3 weeks   • 12 days

5. Did the people in the plane see Linda and Kathy? _____

6. What did the girls use to make a signal for planes?

     • paint   • rocks   • leaves

7. What word did they spell? _____

8. The word was over _____ feet long.

9. What kind of signal did the girls have ready for ships?

     • rocks   • fog   • smoke

10. What made the fire smoke so much?

    • sticks   • green leaves   • bananas

11. What was the name of the ship that rescued the girls?

    • S. S. Mason   • S. S. Milton   • S. S. Sisters

12. Kathy's forehead was hot because she had a _____.

13. How long were the girls on the island?

    • one week   • 2 weeks   • almost 3 weeks

14. How long were the girls on the ocean liner?

    • one week   • 2 weeks   • almost 3 weeks

15. Where did the ocean liner take them? _____

16. Who took them to their new home? _____

17. Did Linda think it would be dull there? _____

18. Linda showed Captain Reeves 4 things that she and Kathy had used to survive on the island. **Underline** those 4 things.

    • machine   • belt buckle   • table   • books

    • TV   • wagon   • house   • socks

    • bathtub   • fish net   • vines

Review Items

19. The temperature inside your body is about _____ degrees when your body is healthy.

20. Most fevers don't go over _____ degrees.

GO TO PART D IN YOUR TEXTBOOK.

A

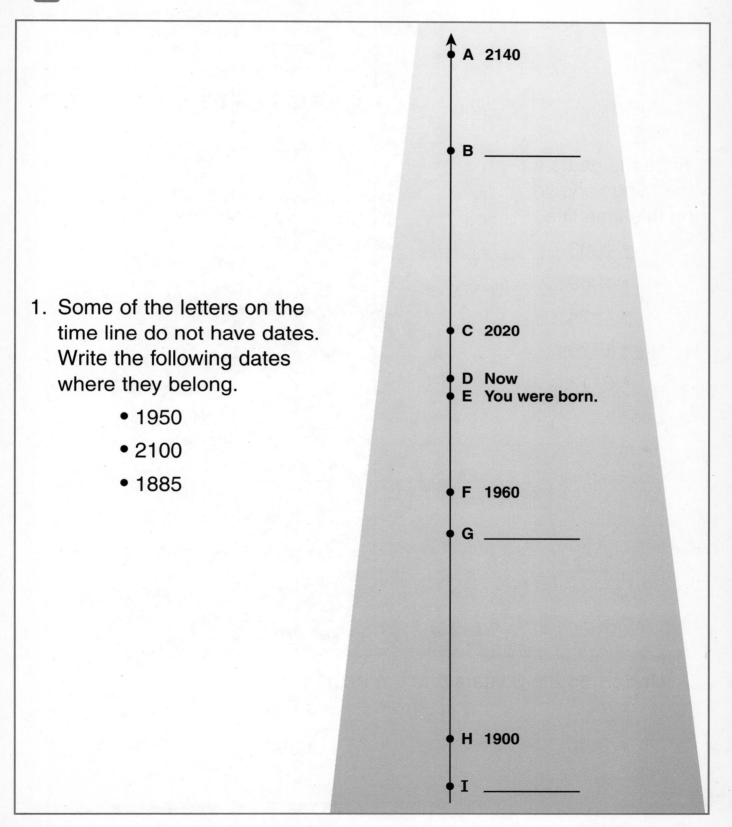

1. Some of the letters on the time line do not have dates. Write the following dates where they belong.

- 1950
- 2100
- 1885

A 2140

B _____

C 2020

D Now

E You were born.

F 1960

G _____

H 1900

I _____

Write the years for the things shown on this time line.

- 1903
- 1969
- 1524
- 1776
- 2113

2. Now _____

3. You were born.

_____

4. Men landed on the

moon. _____

5. The first airplane was

made. _____

6. The United States became

a country. _____

7. **Underline** the 5 years that are in the past.

- 2009
- 1871
- 1994
- 1990
- 2990
- 1490
- 690
- 3690

GO TO PART E IN YOUR TEXTBOOK.

A Story Items

1. Why were Eric and Tom on the mountain?
   - They were cutting down trees.
   - They were picking flowers.
   - They were at a picnic.

2. The time machine looked like a ▨▨▨.
   - giant pile
   - giant pill
   - giant clock

3. How did Tom feel when he saw the time machine?
   - happy
   - scared
   - sad

4. Did Eric feel the same way? _____

5. In what year did Eric and Tom find the time machine? _____

6. What year was Thrig from? _____

7. That year is ▨▨▨.
   - in the past
   - in the future

8. Why couldn't Thrig go back to that year?
   - He was too lazy.
   - He was too weak.
   - He was too busy.

9. What did Eric do that closed the door of the time machine?
   - sat down
   - stood up
   - pulled on a handle

10. What did Eric do to make the time machine move in time?
    - sat down
    - stood up
    - pulled on a handle

Review Items

Write the years for the things shown on this time line.

- 1903
- 1969
- 1524
- 1776
- 2113

11. Now _____

12. You were born.

_____

13. Men landed on the

moon. _____

14. The first airplane was

made. _____

15. The United States became

a country. _____

GO TO PART C IN YOUR TEXTBOOK.

A

1. Look at the years in the list below. **Underline** the 4 years that are in the past.

- 1920   • 1996   • 1790
- 1650   • 2380   • 2560

2. What year did Eric and Tom start their trip? _____

3. What year was Thrig from? _____

4. Thrig was from a year in the ▨.

- past   • future

5. Write 3 years that are in the future.

_____

B **Story Items**

6. The time machine took Eric and Tom to ▨.

- New York
- Japan
- San Francisco

7. How did Eric and Tom find out where they were?

- They asked 3 boys.
- They listened to the radio.
- They found a newspaper.

8. In what year did Tom and Eric see the San Francisco

   earthquake? _____

9. Where did Eric and Tom sleep?

   • in a hotel   • in a barn   • in the street

10. In 1906, most of the streets in San Francisco were ▊▊▊.

    • dirt   • tar   • brick

11. Most of the houses were made of ▊▊▊.

    • brick   • glass   • wood

12. The streetlights were ▊▊▊.

    • not as bright   • brighter

13. **Underline** the 3 items that tell how people got from place to place.

    • horses   • bicycles   • vans
    • trucks   • wagons   • planes

14. Fires started when the ▊▊▊ lines broke.

    • water   • gas   • phone

15. What made the street crack?

    • a flood   • a fire   • an earthquake

16. What happened to Eric at the end of the story?

    _____

    _____

GO TO PART D IN YOUR TEXTBOOK.

1. In what year did Eric and Tom find the time machine? _____

2. What year was Thrig from? _____

3. In what year did Eric fall into an earthquake crack? _____

The time line shows events. Write the year for each event.

• 2400　　• 2100　　• 1900　　• 1906　　• 2 thousand years ago

　　• 5 thousand years ago　　• 1776　　• 1886

4. The year Thrig was from _____

5. Now _____

6. You were born. _____

7. Eric and Tom were in San Francisco. _____

8. The United States became a country. _____

9. Eric and Tom were in Egypt.

_____

B Story Items

10. Where did Eric and Tom go after leaving San Francisco?

   _____

11. Is San Francisco in the United States? _____

12. Is Egypt in the United States? _____

13. When kings and queens of Egypt died, they were buried inside a
   ▬▬ .

   • mummy   • pyramid   • palace

14. **Underline** the 2 things Tom took from the time machine.

   • handle   • clock   • flashlight   • scale

      • dial   • tape recorder   • camera

15. If you remember the things that happened in the story, you have
   learned some rules about the time machine. One rule tells about
   the handle of the time machine. If you pull the handle down, you
   move ▬▬ in time.

      • forward   • backward

16. Another rule has to do with the door of the time machine. When
   you sit down in the seat of the time machine, what happens to

   the door? _____

═══════ GO TO PART E IN YOUR TEXTBOOK. ═══════

A

The time line shows events. Write the year for each event.

1. The year Thrig was from _____

2. Now _____

3. You were born. _____

4. Eric and Tom were in San Francisco. _____

5. The United States became a country. _____

6. Eric and Tom were in Egypt.

_____

B **Story Items**

7. Just before the first soldier appeared, Tom took out his ████ .

   • watch   • radio   • tape recorder   • flashlight

8. Did the soldier speak English? _____

9. Was the soldier friendly? _____

10. Could Tom understand the soldier? _____

11. What did the soldiers in Egypt think Tom was?

      • the sun   • the sun god   • a king

12. How did Tom try to show that he was a sun god?

      • by shining a flashlight

      • by playing a tape recorder

      • by singing sun songs

13. Where did the soldier take Tom and Eric?

      • to the Nile   • to the palace   • in a pyramid

14. What year were Eric and Tom from? _____

Review Items

15. Which arrow shows the way Linda's hand will move? _____

16. Which arrow shows the way the crate will move? _____

GO TO PART E IN YOUR TEXTBOOK.

A

1. When a person makes an object for the first time, the person

_____ the object.

2. The object is called ▨▨.
   - an invention
   - an inventor
   - an airplane

3. Most of the things that we use every day were invented after the year ▨▨.
   - 1800
   - 1900
   - 2200

4. Underline the things that were invented after the year 1800.
   - shoes
   - buildings
   - flashlights
   - doors
   - swords
   - wagons
   - cars

5. **Underline** the 5 things that were not invented by anybody.
   - chairs
   - horses
   - flowers
   - grass
   - planes
   - bottles
   - snakes
   - spiders
   - rugs

B Story Items

6. The people in Egypt did not have cold milk because they didn't have ▨▨.
   - cows
   - goats
   - refrigerators

7. Why didn't the king believe that Tom was a sun god?
   - because the sun wasn't shining
   - because Tom was too young
   - because the flashlight didn't work

Write the years for the things shown on this time line.

8. The year Thrig was from _____

9. Now _____

10. You were born. _____

11. Eric and Tom were in San Francisco. _____

12. The United States became a country. _____

13. Eric and Tom were in Egypt.

_____

14. What did the king do to the flashlight?

   • turned it on   • made it work   • looked at it

15. What year were Eric and Tom from? _____

Review Item

16. Underline the 9 places that are in the United States.

   • Texas   • Chicago   • China
   • Egypt   • Japan   • Lake Michigan
   • Alaska   • Italy   • San Francisco
   • Turkey   • Ohio   • New York City
   • California   • Denver

GO TO PART D IN YOUR TEXTBOOK.

A

1. Write **north, south, east,** and **west** in the boxes to show the directions.

2. Make an **L** where Italy is.

3. Make an **E** where Egypt is.

4. Make a **C** where Greece is.

5. Make a **K** where Turkey is.

6. Greece is ▬▬ of Egypt.

      • north and west   • south and west   • south and east

7. Greece is _____ of Turkey.

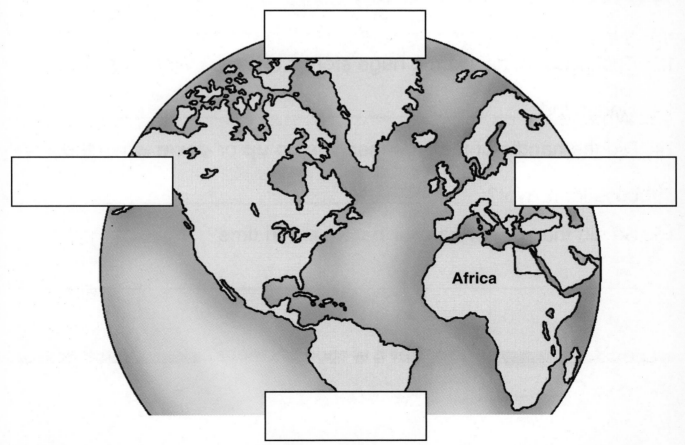

Story Items

8. What did Tom use in this story to make the king think he was a god?

      • flashlight   • radio   • tape recorder

9. Why didn't Tom use the flashlight?

_____

10. Name the river that flowed near the city in Egypt.

_____

11. Which is the smarter way to move grain—by wagons or by raft?

_____

12. Why didn't the people in Egypt use trucks to haul things?

_____

13. Eric and Tom saw some huge stones on rafts. What were the

stones for? _____

14. Did the handle of the time machine go **up** or **down** when the

boys left Egypt? _____

15. So did they go **forward** or **backward** in time?

_____

GO TO PART D IN YOUR TEXTBOOK.

A

1. Part of Greece went to war with _____.

2. The war began because a queen from _____

   ran away with a man from _____.

3. ■■■ ships went to war against Troy.
   - A hundred   • A thousand   • A million

4. How long did the war last? _____

5. What kept the soldiers from getting inside Troy?

   _____

6. At last, the Greek army built a _____.

7. What was inside this object? _____

8. What did the men do at night?
   - slept   • opened the gate   • rang a bell

B **Story Items**

9. Where did the time machine take Eric and Tom after they left Egypt?
   - Turkey   • Greece   • Troy

10. Is Greece in the United States? _____

11. What was the teacher in the story wearing?

    • a suit

    • a robe

    • a cape

12. The teacher wanted the students to argue so they would learn
    to ▮▮▮.

    • fight

    • think clearly

    • make long speeches

13. Where were the ships going? _____

14. At the end of the story, Eric and Tom left Greece. Which way did
    they move the handle in the time machine—up or down?

    _____

15. So will they go **forward** in time or **backward** in time?

    _____

16. Will they go very far in time? _____

GO TO PART D IN YOUR TEXTBOOK.

A

1. **Underline** 3 things that were true of humans 40 thousand years ago.

- They lived in houses.
- They wore animal skins.
- They wore hats.
- They were taller than people of today.
- They were shorter than people of today.

- They rode bikes.
- They lived in caves.

B **Story Items**

2. The force on Eric and Tom was very great when they left Greece because the time machine ▮▮▮.

- was broken
- was on a mountain
- went very far back in time

3. How far back in time were the boys in this story?

- 40 thousand years
- 4 thousand years
- 5 thousand years
- 3 thousand years

4. **Underline** 3 kinds of animals the boys saw 40 thousand years ago.

- lions
- saber-toothed tigers
- horses
- bears
- alligators
- mammoths
- cows

5. **Underline** 2 ways a mammoth was different from an elephant of today.

- short tusks
- long tusks
- short hair
- long hair

6. **Underline** 2 ways a saber-toothed tiger was different from a tiger of today.

- no ears   - no teeth   - long teeth
- long tail   - short tail

7. The door of the time machine wouldn't close because

_____.

8. What scared the mammoth away? _____

9. Some humans ran toward the time machine. What were those

humans wearing? _____

10. What was Tom trying to do with the long branch?

- hit the humans   - straighten the bent door
- move the seat

Review Items

11. Which picture shows the largest force? _____

12. Which picture shows the smallest force? _____

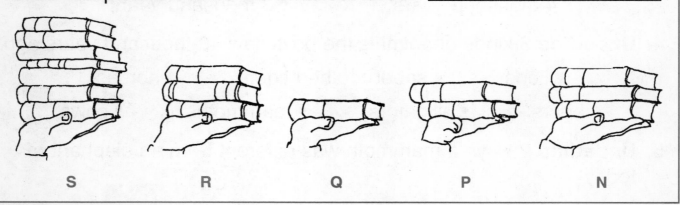

S   R   Q   P   N

GO TO PART D IN YOUR TEXTBOOK.

A

Write the time for each event shown on the time line.

- 3 thousand years ago
- 4 thousand years in the future
- 40 thousand years ago

1. Eric and Tom were in the city of the future.

_____

2. The year Thrig was from _____

3. Now _____

4. You were born. _____

5. Eric and Tom were in San Francisco. _____

6. The United States became a country. _____

7. Greece and Troy went to war.

_____

8. Eric and Tom were in Egypt.

_____

9. Eric and Tom saw a saber-toothed tiger.

_____

B Story Items

10. Where did Eric and Tom go after they left the cave people?

    • San Francisco   • Turkey   • city of the future

11. About how many years from now were Tom and Eric in the city of the future?

    • 400 years   • 40 thousand years   • 4 thousand years

12. Could all the people in the city understand Eric and Tom? _____

13. Why could the old man understand them?

    • He studied old machines.

    • He studied old languages.

    • He studied old people.

14. The people in the city of the future did not fix their machines.

    What fixed their machines? _____

15. Eric and Tom couldn't get a machine that would help them work their time machine because their time machine was ▆▆▆ .

    • too big   • too old   • too heavy

16. Why did the people of the future use such simple language?

    • They didn't think much.

    • They didn't have much time.

    • They didn't have any schools.

17. After Eric and Tom left the city of the future, they saw a ship. Was it a **modern ship** or was it an **old-time ship?**

    _____

GO TO PART D IN YOUR TEXTBOOK.

A Story Items

1. Where did Eric and Tom go after leaving the city of the future?

   _____

2. Who discovered America? _____

3. When did he discover America? _____

4. Is Spain in the United States? _____

5. In what year were Eric and Tom in Spain? _____

6. Is the world round or flat? _____

7. Did Columbus think the world was round or flat? _____

8. Did the fat man think the world was round or flat? _____

9. The fat man thought that if Columbus sailed to America his ships would ▉▉▉▉.

   - go downhill
   - get caught in whirlpools
   - sail off the edge of the earth

10. What went into the time machine at the end of the story?

    _____

11. The fat man didn't like the dog because ▉▉▉▉.

    - the dog was white
    - the dog bit a worker
    - the dog ate wood

Review Items

12. Write **north, south, east,** and **west** in the boxes to show the directions.
13. Greece is ________________ of Turkey.
14. Greece is ▬ of Egypt.
    - south and east
    - south and west
    - north and west

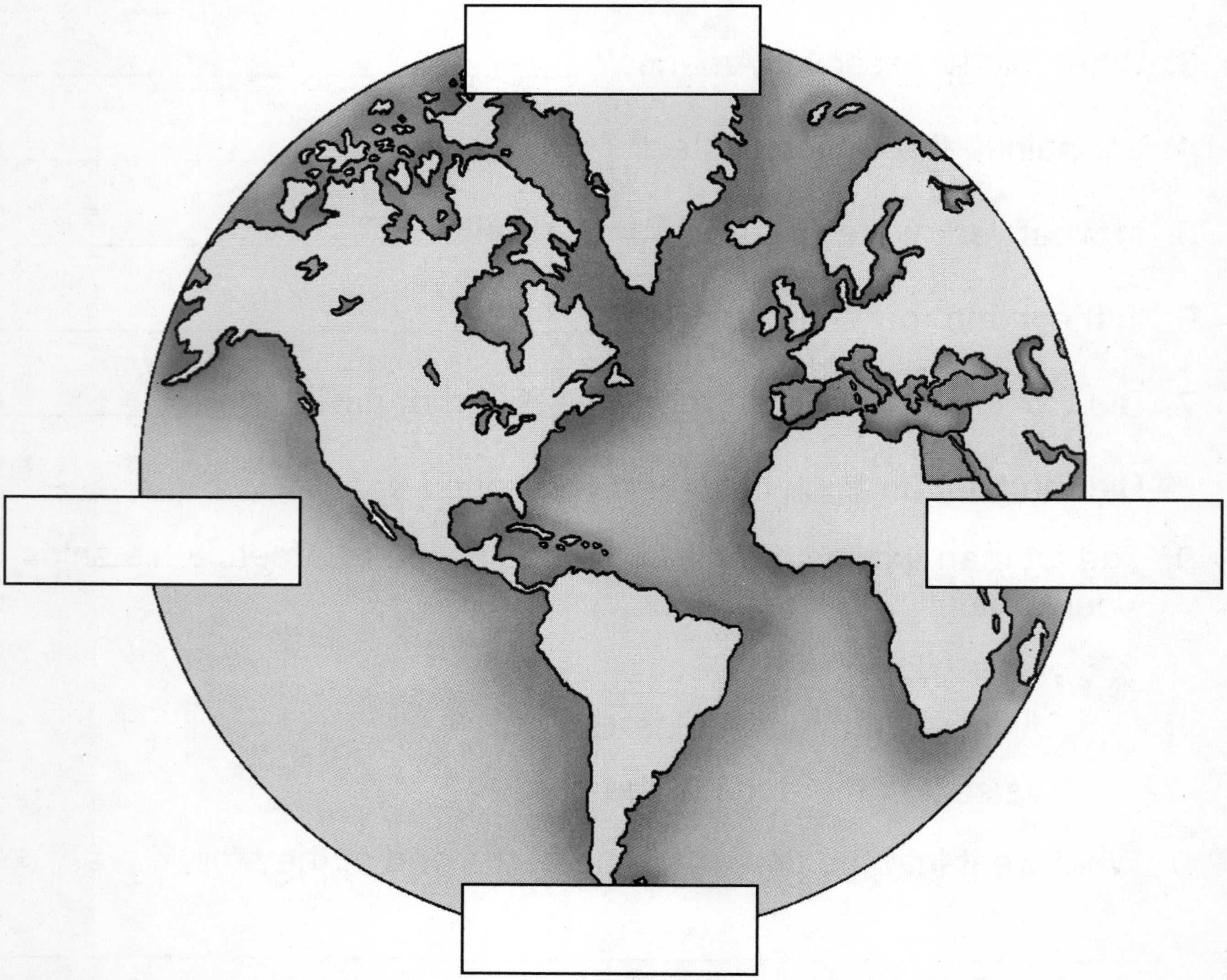

GO TO PART E IN YOUR TEXTBOOK.

A

Write the time for each event shown on the time line.

1. **Eric and Tom were in the city of the future.**

   _____

2. **The year Thrig was from** _____

3. **Now** _____

4. **You were born.** _____

5. **Eric and Tom were in San Francisco.** _____

6. **The United States became a country.** _____

7. **Columbus discovered America.** _____

8. **Greece and Troy went to war.**

   _____

9. **Eric and Tom were in Egypt.**

   _____

10. **Eric and Tom saw a saber-toothed tiger.**

    _____

B   Story Items

11. Who did the dog like—Eric or Tom? _____

12. The fat man ran away from the time machine because he was ▓▓▓.

    • hungry   • frightened   • in a hurry

13. Eric wanted to take the dog with them in the time machine because he was afraid that the soldiers would ▓▓▓.

    • hurt the dog   • hurt the fat man

    • steal the time machine

14. Which way did Tom move the handle when they left Spain?

    _____

15. Did he move the handle in the right direction? _____

16. Did Eric and Tom go forward in time or backward in time?

    _____

17. The boys saw a ship when the door of the time machine opened. What kind of ship was it?

    • a Greek ship

    • a ship that Columbus sailed

    • a Viking ship

───────── **GO TO PART D IN YOUR TEXTBOOK.** ─────────

A Story Items

1. Tom and Eric found a dog in Spain. Write **3** things that tell what

   the dog looked like. _____

   _____

2. Which way did Tom move the handle when they left Spain?

   _____

3. Did he move the handle in the right direction? _____

4. Did the boys go **forward** in time or **backward** in time?

   _____

5. After the boys left Spain, they saw a ship when the door of the
   time machine opened. What kind of ship was it?

   _____

6. In what year were Eric and Tom in the Land of the Vikings?

   _____

Here are some things the Vikings said:

   • Su urf.   • Ul fas e mern.   • Left ingra.

7. **Circle** the words that mean **Come with me.**
8. **Underline** the words that mean **I like that.**
9. **Make a box** around the words that mean **Danger, danger.**

10. Why couldn't Eric and Tom understand what the Vikings said?
- They didn't speak.   • Their language was different.
- They talked too fast.

11. **Underline** 2 things that tell what the Vikings wore.
- animal skins   • glasses   • helmets   • slippers

12. Why did the Vikings like Tom and Eric's dog?
- It beat their best dog.   • It was white.
- It was hungry.

13. The boys were eating inside the large building. How many

windows were in that building? _____

14. What did the Vikings use to eat their meat? _____

15. Which direction do you go to get from Italy to the Land of the

Vikings? _____

Review Item

16. **Underline** 3 things that were true of humans 40 thousand years ago.
- a. They wore hats.
- b. They were shorter than people of today.
- c. They lived in caves.
- d. They drove cars.
- e. They lived in pyramids.
- f. They rode bikes.
- g. They were taller than people of today.
- h. They wore animal skins.

GO TO PART D IN YOUR TEXTBOOK.

A

1. What year were Eric and Tom from? _____

2. About how many years in our future is the city of the future?

   _____

3. What year was Thrig from? _____

4. In what year were Eric and Tom in San Francisco? _____

5. In what year did Columbus discover America? _____

6. In what year were Eric and Tom in the Land of the Vikings?

   _____

7. How far back in time were Eric and Tom when they were in

   Greece? _____

8. How far back in time were Eric and Tom when they were in

   Egypt? _____

9. How far back in time were Eric and Tom when they saw the cave

   people? _____

B **Story Items**

10. Tom and Eric ate inside a large building. How many windows

    were in that building? _____

11. The Vikings from the other village wore ▬▬.

 • leg bands • head bands • arm bands

12. What did Tom use to stop the fighting?

 • tape recorder • radio • flashlight

13. Tom said he was the god of _____.

14. Which way did Tom move the handle when the boys left the Land

 of the Vikings? _____

15. Did they go forward in time or back in time? _____

16. What season was it when the door of the time machine opened?

_____

17. What was Tom looking for when he left the time machine?

 • people • animals • snow

18. What did Tom hear when he was in the grove?

 • Vikings • bells • people

19. Why did Tom get lost on his way back to the time machine?

_____

═══════════ **GO TO PART D IN YOUR TEXTBOOK.** ═══════════

A

1. The United States used to be part of ▇▇▇.

   • Spain   • England   • Italy

2. When the United States announced that it was a country, England went to war with the United States. Who was the leader of the United States Army during the war?

   • George Wilson   • Abe Lincoln

   • George Washington

3. Which country won the war? _____

4. Who was the first president of the United States?

   _____

5. Who is the president of the United States today?

   _____

B **Story Items**

6. In the Land of the Vikings, what did Tom use to stop the fighting?

   _____

7. After leaving the Land of the Vikings, did the boys go **forward** in

   time or **backward** in time? _____

8. What was Tom looking for when he left the time machine?

   • people   • food   • warm clothes

9. Why did Tom get lost on his way back to the time machine?

_____

10. In what year were Eric and Tom in Concord? _____

11. Is Concord in the United States? _____

12. When Eric and Tom were in Concord, the United States was at war. Which country was winning that war in 1777?

_____

13. Who led Tom and Robert to Eric? _____

14. Tom and Eric could understand the people in Concord. Tell why.

_____

15. The English soldiers were looking for spies. What would they do

to spies that they found? _____

16. The English soldiers were shooting at Tom, Eric, and Robert because the soldiers thought that they were shooting at ▉▉▉.
    - Vikings   • an enemy   • friends

17. The English soldiers wore ▉▉▉ coats.
    - long   • warm   • red

GO TO PART D IN YOUR TEXTBOOK.

A

Write the time for each event shown on the time line.

1. Eric and Tom were in the city of the future.

   _____

2. The year Thrig was from _____

3. Now _____

4. You were born. _____

5. Eric and Tom were in San Francisco. _____

6. Eric and Tom were in Concord. _____

7. The United States became a country. _____

8. Columbus discovered America. _____

9. Eric and Tom were in the land of the Vikings. _____

10. Greece and Troy went to war.

    _____

11. Eric and Tom were in Egypt.

    _____

12. Eric and Tom saw a saber-toothed tiger.

    _____

13. Who led Eric, Tom, and Robert to the time machine?

_____

14. Robert decided not to go with Eric and Tom. What was he going to do?

   • join the English army   • join Washington's army

              • become president

15. The door of the time machine wouldn't close because something

   was frozen. What was frozen? _____

16. What was inside the door on the dashboard?

   • a tape recorder   • a microphone   • a flashlight

17. Did Tom and Eric tell the other kids where they got the dog?

_____

18. What did Tom and Eric name the dog? _____

━━━━━━━━━━━━━ **GO TO PART D IN YOUR TEXTBOOK.** ━━━━━━━━━━━━━

A

1. If you go east from Australia, what ocean do you go through?

_____

2. If you go west from the United States, what ocean do you go

through? _____

B **Story Items**

3. Name the country where this part of the story takes place.

_____

4. What is a group of kangaroos called? _____

5. The mob moved from place to place when the mob ran out
of ▆▆▆.

   • grass and weeds   • water and grass   • gas and food

6. How do you know Toby wasn't very important in the mob?

   • He was at the front of the mob.

   • He was not in a mob.

   • He was at the back of the mob.

7. What is a baby kangaroo called? _____

8. Name the only 2 things Toby liked to do.

_____

9. Did Toby's mother like Toby? _____

10. Did Toby like to be called a joey? _____

11. Write the letter of the most important kangaroo in the mob. _____

12. Write the letter of Toby. _____

13. Write the letter of a kangaroo that is almost as important as the

    leader. _____

14. Write the letter of a kangaroo that is a little more important than

    Toby. _____

GO TO PART D IN YOUR TEXTBOOK.

A

1. What is the only country that has wild kangaroos?
   - America
   - Canada
   - Australia

2. Big kangaroos grow to be as big as a _____.

3. Small kangaroos grow to be no bigger than a ▬▬▬.
   - cow
   - beagle
   - moose

4. How long is a kangaroo when it is born? _____

5. Where does a baby kangaroo live right after it is born?

   _____

6. How long does it live there? _____

7. How far can a kangaroo go in one jump? _____

B Story Items

8. A kangaroo that sits on a hill and warns the mob when trouble is

   coming is called a _____.

9. What does that animal do if there's trouble?
   - waves its tail
   - stamps its foot
   - screams

10. Who told Toby he had to be a lookout? _____

11. Where did Toby go to be a lookout? _____

   _____

12. When Toby was a tiny kangaroo, hunters caught his father. What job did his father have when he was caught?

_____

13. Why did Toby's father get caught? _____

_____

14. Where did some kangaroos think Toby's father was now?

  • on the other side of Australia

  • on the other side of the Pacific Ocean

  • on the other side of Turkey

15. Toby's father had a tail that was different from any other kangaroo's tail. Name 2 ways that his father's tail was different.

_____

_____

16. After Toby got to the top of the hill, he did something he didn't

mean to do. What was that? _____

17. Who did Toby hear at the end of the story? _____

GO TO PART D IN YOUR TEXTBOOK.

A

1. A peacock is a large ▮▮▮.

    • fish   • dog   • bird

2. The feathers of a male peacock are different from the feathers of other birds. **Underline** 2 ways they are different.

    • longer   • stronger   • more colorful

    • older   • shorter

3. Do peacocks live as wild animals in Australia? _____

4. Which is more beautiful—a peacock's feathers or a peacock's

    voice? _____

5. What does a male peacock spread when it shows off?

    _____

6. How long is a full-grown peacock from its head to the end of its

    tail? _____

B Story Items

7. Name the leader of the hunters. _____

8. About how far was it from the mob to the ship? _____

9. What country was Mabel from? _____

10. In that country, Mabel ran a large _____.

11. **Underline** 2 kinds of animals Mabel wanted to catch in Australia.

    • peacocks   • koalas   • platypuses

    • camels   • elephants   • kangaroos

    • cuckoos

12. Mabel didn't plan to keep all the animals she caught. What was she going to do with the animals she didn't keep?

_____

13. What did Toby do to signal the mob about the hunters?

    • smacked his tail   • smacked his foot

           • smacked his lips

14. After Toby's first signal, the mob stood still. What did the mob do

after Toby's second signal? _____

15. What happened to Toby at the end of the story? _____

_____

16. The hunters hoped to get 5 kangaroos. How many did they

catch? _____

17. Who saved the other kangaroos? _____

════ GO TO PART D IN YOUR TEXTBOOK. ════

1. How many seconds are in one minute? _____

2. Some clocks have a hand that counts seconds. When that hand
   goes all the way around the clock, how much time has passed?

   • one hour   • one minute   • one second

3. The second hand on a clock went around 2 times. How much

   time passed? _____

4. What do we call the things that a ship carries? _____

Look at the picture of the ship. Write one of these names on
each line:

   • stern   • hold   • deck   • bulkhead   • bow

5. _____

6. _____

7. _____

8. _____   9. _____

10. What do we call the part of the ship where the cargo is carried?

_____

C Story Items

11. About how far did the sailors have to carry Toby? _____

12. What time of day was it when Toby reached the ship?
    - morning   - noon   - evening

13. Name the part of the ship where the sailors threw Toby.

_____

14. Why couldn't Toby see when he first got there? _____

_____

15. What did Toby smell? _____

16. Name the country that is just north of the United States.

_____

17. Name 2 kinds of animals that were locked up with Toby.

_____

18. Which animal was showing off? _____

19. Where did that animal come from?
    - China   - Turkey   - India

20. Name the country the ship is going to. _____

GO TO PART E IN YOUR TEXTBOOK.

A Skill Items

Here are three events that happened in the story:

    a. The police boat left and one of the sailors untied the animals.

    b. Pip told the other animals that the trip to Canada would take 10 days.

    c. The sailors tied up the animals and covered them with blankets.

1. Write the letter of the event that happened near the beginning of the story. _____

2. Write the letter of the event that happened in the middle of the story. _____

3. Write the letter of the event that happened near the end of the story. _____

B Story Items

4. In what country are peacocks wild animals? _____

5. Where was the ship when Toby got on it? _____

6. Name the country the ship was going to. _____

7. How long would that trip take? _____

8. What ocean was the ship crossing? _____

9. How did Mabel and the captain break the law in Australia?

  • hunting peacocks   • hunting lions

        • hunting on a game preserve

10. Pip wanted the captain to stand behind him so that Pip would look ▬▬.

        • ugly   • old   • beautiful

11. What did the captain drop over Pip? _____

12. Why was Toby happy when he saw the police boat?

    • He thought he would be saved.

    • He thought Mabel was coming.

    • He thought the captain was leaving.

13. Did the peacock think that the police would help the animals?

    _____

14. What was the police officer supposed to look at?

    • the stern   • the cargo   • the captain

15. What was the real cargo? _____

16. What did Mabel say their cargo was? _____

17. Did Mabel lie about the cargo? _____

GO TO PART C IN YOUR TEXTBOOK.

A **Skill Items**

Here are three events that happened in the story:

 a. The sailors put Toby on a cart.   b. The ship docked in Canada.
    c. Mabel took Toby to a circus.

1. Write the letter of the event that happened near the beginning of

   the story. _____

2. Write the letter of the event that happened in the middle of the

   story. _____

3. Write the letter of the event that happened near the end of the

   story. _____

B

4. Which direction would you go to get from the main part of the

   United States to Canada? _____

5. Which country is **larger**—Canada or the United States?

   _____

6. Where do **more** people live—in Canada or in the United States?

   _____

7. Which country is **warmer**—Canada or the United States?

   _____

8. Write **north, south, east,** and **west** in the right boxes.

9. Make an **A** on Canada.

10. Make a **T** on the United States.

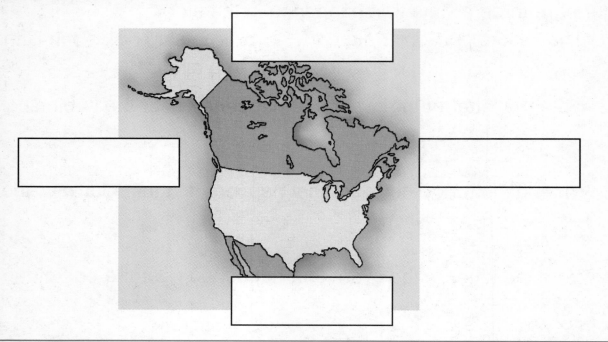

C **Story Items**

11. Name the country where the ship docked. _____

12. What time was it when they docked?

      • afternoon   • evening   • night

13. Where did the truck take Toby? _____

14. What will he do there?

          • shoot a cannon   • drive a truck

              • get shot from a cannon

15. How did Toby feel at the end of the story? _____

GO TO PART D IN YOUR TEXTBOOK.

A Skill Items

Here are three events that happened in the story:
   a. The owner took Toby into a tent.
   b. Two boys threw papers at Toby.
   c. The owner told Toby to ride a bicycle backward on the high wire.

1. Write the letter of the event that happened near the beginning of the story. _____

2. Write the letter of the event that happened in the middle of the story. _____

3. Write the letter of the event that happened near the end of the story. _____

B

4. **Underline** the place where a circus is sometimes held.
   • a train   • a tent   • a store

5. Are all the acts on the ground? _____

C Story Items

6. The owner told Toby that he had to do tricks if he wanted

_____.

7. Was Toby part of a good circus? _____

8. Was Toby the only animal in the circus? _____

9. About how many people were in the stands? _____

Here are the announcements the owner made:
    a. Toby will ride a bicycle backward on the floor.
    b. Toby will ride a bicycle forward on the floor.
    c. Toby will ride a bicycle backward on the high wire.
    d. Toby will walk with the bicycle on the floor.

10. Write the letter of the first announcement the owner made. _____

11. Write the letter of the second announcement the owner

    made. _____

12. Write the letter of the third announcement the owner made. _____

13. Write the letter of the fourth announcement the owner made. _____

14. Write the letter of the easiest trick. _____

15. The owner told Toby to do different tricks. Which was easier, the

    first trick or the second trick? _____

16. Did Toby do any tricks? _____

17. Will Toby get any food from the circus owner? _____

━━━━━━━━━━━ **GO TO PART D IN YOUR TEXTBOOK.** ━━━━━━━━━━━

A

1. Boxers wear large mittens when they box. What are those

   mittens called? _____

2. What do we call the place where boxers box?

   • a rink   • a ring   • a square

3. Is that place round? _____

4. What do the boxers do with the gloves? _____

   _____

B **Story Items**

5. The circus owner told Toby that he had to do tricks if he wanted

   _____.

6. Was Toby part of a good circus? _____

7. Why did the owner refund the people's money?

   • because it rained   • because the circus closed

   • because Toby did not do any tricks

8. The owner didn't give Toby any food. Tell why. _____

   _____

9. How much did the circus owner pay for Toby?

   _____

10. How much did Mabel pay the owner when she bought Toby

    back? _____

11. Who made the best deal, Mabel or the owner? _____

12. Where did Mabel take Toby after she bought him back?
    • Roadside Zoo   • Roadside Cafe   • City Zoo

13. Did she make money when she sold Toby the second time?

    _____

14. Toby recognized his father by looking at his _____.

Review Items

15. Write the letter **A** on Australia.

16. Write the letter **B** on the United States.

17. Write the letter **C** on Canada.

18. Write the letter **D** on the Pacific Ocean.

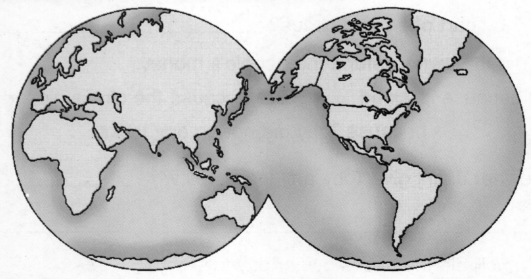

A Story Items

1. Who were the boxing kangaroos? ____________________

2. Who did the kangaroos hit? ____________________

3. Did the crowd like this act? ____________________

4. Why didn't the crowd listen to Toby?
   - People were clapping and yelling.
   - People were sleeping.
   - People were eating.

5. Who made the crowd become quiet? ____________________

6. Who told the police where to find Mabel and the captain?

   ____

7. What happened to Mabel and the captain?

   ____

8. Pip decided to stay in Canada so he could ____.
   - open a zoo
   - entertain people
   - box with kangaroos

9. Name the country that Toby and his father went to at the end of the story. ____________________

10. Why did the other kangaroos shout, "Hooray for Toby"?

    ____

11. Make an **L** on the leader of the mob.

12. Make a **T** on Toby.

13. Make an **F** on Toby's father.

14. Make an **M** on Toby's mother.

Review Items

15. Why did the circus owner refund the people's money?

_____

16. How much did the circus owner pay for Toby?

_____

17. How much did Mabel pay the circus owner when she bought

Toby back? _____

GO TO PART C IN YOUR TEXTBOOK.

A

1. Things closer to the bottom of the pile

   went into the pile _____.

2. Which object went into the pile **first?**

   _____

3. Which object went into the pile **last?**

   _____

4. Which object went into the pile **earlier—**

   the knife or the book? _____

5. Which object went into the pile **earlier—**

   the pencil or the cup? _____

6. Which object went into the pile just **after**

   the bone? _____

7. Which object went into the pile just **after**

   the pencil? _____

B **Story Items**

8. Which came earlier on Earth, dinosaurs or horses?

   _____

9. Which came earlier on Earth, strange sea animals or dinosaurs?

_____

10. What kind of animals lived in the Mesozoic?

_____

Use these names to answer the questions: **Tyrannosaurus, Triceratops.**

11. What is animal A? _____

12. What is animal B? _____

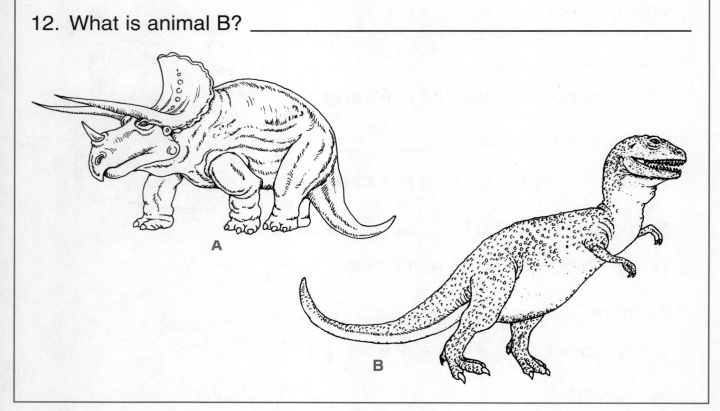

A

B

GO TO PART D IN YOUR TEXTBOOK.

A Story Items

1. How old was Edna Parker? _____

2. How did Edna usually feel on the ship?

   • happy   • bored   • nervous

3. Why wouldn't Edna be bored on this trip?

   _____

4. Where was the ship starting from? _____

5. Where was it going? _____

6. How far was the trip? _____

7. How long would it take?

   • more than one day   • one day   • less than one day

8. Draw an **arrow** on the map below to show the trip.

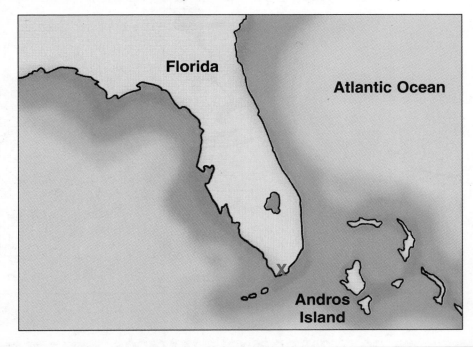

9. The ship would pass through a place where hundreds of ships have sunk or been lost. Name that place.

_____

10. **Underline** the 3 things you find in the Bermuda Triangle.

- huge waves
- mountains
- streams
- whirlpools
- sudden storms
- icebergs

11. As the girls left the map room, Captain Parker told them to stay

away from the sides of the ship and the _____.

Review Items

Use these names to answer the questions: **Tyrannosaurus, Triceratops.**

12. What is animal A? _____

13. What is animal B? _____

A

B

GO TO PART C IN YOUR TEXTBOOK.

A

1. What are clouds made of? _____

2. What kind of cloud does picture A show? _____

3. Write the letter of the clouds that may stay in the sky for days at

   a time. _____

A

B

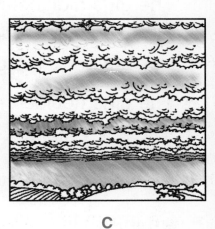
C

4. Write the letter of the storm clouds. _____

5. Write the letter of the clouds that have frozen drops of

   water. _____

6. Write the letter of the clouds that may be five miles high. _____

B **Story Items**

7. How old was Edna Parker? _____

8. How did Edna usually feel on the ship?

   • happy   • bored   • nervous

9. As the girls left the map room, Captain Parker told them to stay

away from the _____

and the _____.

10. Why didn't the girls stay in the galley?

 • The cook complained about his tooth.

 • It was dirty.

 • It smelled bad.

11. The girls didn't stay in the engine room because the engineer told them that they would have to ▮▮▮▮.

 • go to the galley   • work   • sing

12. The girls decided not to climb the ▮▮▮▮.

 • stairs   • mast   • flag pole

13. Did any of the crew members play with Edna and Carla? _____

14. Carla wanted to pretend that they were ▮▮▮▮.

 • on an island   • on their own ship

 • on top of a mountain

15. Who told them to stay away from the lifeboats?

_____

16. Which girl wanted to play in the lifeboat? _____

17. How many crew members were watching while Edna and Carla

talked about playing in the lifeboat? _____

GO TO PART D IN YOUR TEXTBOOK.

A **Story items**

1. When today's story began, Edna and Carla were pretending they

   had their own ship. Who was the captain? _____

2. **Underline** 3 things the first mate did to look more like a sailor.

   - took off her shoes

   - wore a sailor suit

   - wore short pants

   - rolled up her pants

   - wrapped a handkerchief around her head

3. What happened to the lifeboat when the girls were in it?

   - It dropped into the water.

   - It turned over.

   - It rang a bell.

4. What part of the lifeboat hit the water first, the bow or the stern?

   _____

5. What happened to Edna when the boat hit the water?

   - She fell out of the boat.   • She bumped into Carla.

                    • She hit her head.

6. What 2 things did the girls do so the people on the large ship

   would notice them? _____

   _____

7. Did anyone notice them? _____

8. When Edna and Carla turned around, they saw one of these

   clouds. Write the letter of that cloud. _____

A

B

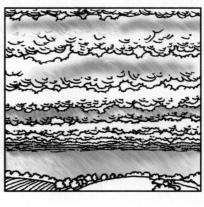

C

9. When the girls started bailing, there was about _____
   inches of water in the boat.

10. What made the girls stop bailing?

   • a whirlpool   • a wind   • an airplane

11. At the end of the story, how high were the waves?

   _____

12. How fast were the winds moving?

   _____

GO TO PART C IN YOUR TEXTBOOK.

A

1. What happens to a drop at B?

   • It freezes.   • It moves up.   • It gets smaller.

2. Draw 2 arrows in picture 1 to show how hail is formed in a storm cloud.

3. If you break a hailstone in half, what will you see inside the

   hailstone? _____

4. Picture 2 shows half of a hailstone. How many times did the

   stone go through a cloud? _____

PICTURE 1

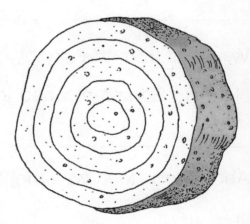

PICTURE 2

B **Story Items**

5. What happened to the lifeboat when the girls got in it?

_____

6. At the end of the last story, how high were the waves?

_____

7. When today's story began, Carla shouted that she saw land.

What did she really see? _____

8. When could Edna see in the distance?
   - at the top of a wave
   - at the bottom of a wave

9. After the giant wave hit, the boat was being sucked into a

_____.

10. Some things happened so fast that Carla and Edna had to try to figure out what they were. What made the blinding flash?

_____

11. What fell from the sky? _____

12. How did Edna feel when the sea was calm again?

_____

13. About how deep was the water when Edna stepped out of the

lifeboat? _____

14. About how far was it from the lifeboat to the beach?

_____

GO TO PART D IN YOUR TEXTBOOK.

A Story Items

1. After the giant wave hit the boat in the last story, what was the

   boat being sucked into? _____

2. Some things happened so fast that Carla and Edna had to try to
   figure out what they were. What made the blinding flash?

   _____

3. What fell from the sky? _____

4. About how far was it from the lifeboat to the beach?

   _____

5. What was right behind the beach? _____

6. What was strange about the sand on the beach?

   _____

7. Edna and Carla woke up when it was dark. What woke them

   up? _____

8. The animal Edna saw was as big as some of the

   _____.

9. Did the animal walk on 4 legs or 2 legs? _____

10. Where did the girls go to spend the last part of the night?

    _____

11. Did the girls get much sleep? _____

12. What was the first thing the girls discovered in the red sand?

_____.

13. The footprints were ▬▬ long.
- a foot
- a yard
- half a meter

Review Items

14. How many inches long is a yard? _____

15. About how many inches long is a meter? _____

16. Which direction would you go to get from Canada to the main

part of the United States? _____

17. Which country is larger, Canada or the United States?

_____

18. Which country is colder, Canada or the United States?

_____

19. Where do more people live, in Canada or in the United States?

_____

20. The picture shows half a hailstone. How many times did the stone go through a

cloud? _____

GO TO PART C IN YOUR TEXTBOOK.

A Story Items

1. What was strange about the sand on the beach where Edna and

   Carla landed? _____

2. The footprints of the animal were _____ long.

3. How many toes did each footprint have? _____

4. What did the size of the footprints tell about the size of the animal?

   • It was bigger than a bear.

   • It was a bear.

   • It was smaller than a bear.

5. How did Edna know that the animal was very heavy?

   • The footprints were long.

   • The footprints made deep dents.

   • The footprints had 3 toes.

6. What part of the animal made the deep groove between the

   footprints? _____

7. Edna wasn't sure if she wanted to follow the animal. **Underline** 2
   things that tell what the parts of her mind wanted to do.

   • read about dinosaurs

   • run

   • think

   • learn more about the animal

   • find something to eat

8. Edna saw something next to the path that she recognized from a picture in a book. What did she see?

   • a stream   • a tree   • a bug

9. What else was in that picture?

   • dinosaurs   • ships   • rocks

10. How did that make her feel? _____

---

11. Write the letter of the footprint made by the heaviest animal. _____

12. Write the letter of the footprint made by the lightest animal. _____

The picture shows marks left by an animal.

13. Make an arrow from dot A to show the direction the animal is moving.

14. Write the letter of the part that shows a footprint. _____

15. Write the letter of the part that shows the mark left by the

    animal's tail. _____

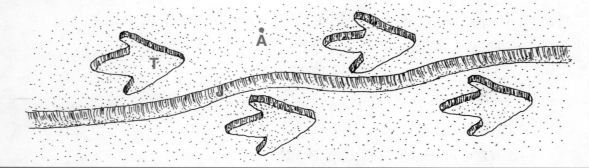

GO TO PART C IN YOUR TEXTBOOK.

A **Story Items**

1. Edna and Carla saw a winged animal. Was that animal a bird?

_____

2. How do you know?

> • It had teeth.   • It didn't have a beak.

> • It didn't have feathers.

3. Its wings were covered with something that looked like ▇▇▇.

> • feathers   • leather   • hair

4. **Underline** the answer. How long ago did those winged animals live on Earth?

> • a thousand years ago

> • a million years ago

> • a hundred million years ago

5. **Underline** the name of the dinosaur the girls saw.

> • Triceratops   • Mammoth   • Tyrannosaurus

6. What cracked the tree that Edna was hiding behind?

> • Tyrannosaurus's head   • Tyrannosaurus's foot

> • Tyrannosaurus's tail

7. What happened to Edna when the tree cracked?

_____

8. Before Edna started to run, she heard noises from the clearing. What made the leathery flapping sound?

> • Tyrannosaurus   • the flying dinosaur   • Carla

9. Whose bones were making the crunching sound?

_____

10. Tyrannosaurus didn't hear Edna running because it was .

   • sleeping   • eating   • scratching

11. As Edna ran through the jungle toward the beach, what did she

   see on the path? _____

12. Did Edna slow down when she saw it? _____

13. When Edna got to the beach, she realized that something was

   wrong. What was wrong? _____

Review Items

The speedometers are in two different cars.

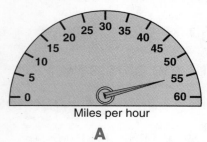

A

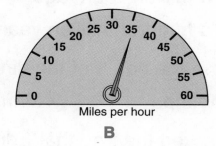

B

14. How fast is car A going? _____

15. How fast is car B going? _____

16. Which car is going faster? _____

GO TO PART C IN YOUR TEXTBOOK.

A Story Items

1. At the beginning of the story, Edna was trying to decide something. **Underline** what she was trying to decide.

    - whether she should go back into the jungle

    - whether she should hide under the boat

    - whether she should call for help

2. Edna didn't call to Carla because the sound might ▆▆▆.

    - make the birds fly   • not be loud enough

           • catch the dinosaur's attention

3. When Edna was near the clearing, she couldn't see Tyrannosaurus. Underline 2 ways she knew that Tyrannosaurus was nearby.

    - She could feel its skin.

    - She could hear it.

    - She could smell it.

    - She could taste it.

4. Carla was lying very still because ▆▆▆.

    - Tyrannosaurus was near   • the leaves were wet

           • Edna was watching

5. What happened to Carla's leg? _____

    _____

6. Edna made up a plan to save Carla. How was Edna going to

    catch Tyrannosaurus's attention? _____

    _____

7. In Edna's plan, what would Tyrannosaurus do?

   _____

8. What would Carla do? _____

   _____

9. Did Edna get to try her plan? _____

10. What came into the clearing when Tyrannosaurus was moving

    back and forth? _____

11. What were Edna and Carla trying to do at the end of the story?

    _____

Review Items

12. Which object is the hottest? _____

13. What is the temperature of that object? _____

14. Which object is the coldest? _____

15. What is the temperature of that object? _____

A

20 degrees

B

60 degrees

C

35 degrees

GO TO PART C IN YOUR TEXTBOOK.

A

1. What comes out of a volcano? _____

2. Draw arrows at **A,** at **B,** and at **C** to show the way the melted rock moves.

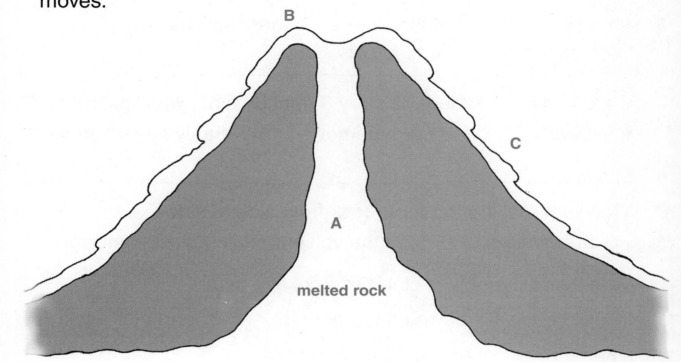

B

C

A

melted rock

3. Two things happen to melted rock when it moves down the sides of a volcano. **Underline** those 2 things.

- It gets hotter.
- It gets cooler.
- It gets harder.
- It runs faster.
- It gets softer.

4. What is it called when the earth shakes and cracks?

_____

B **Story Items**

5. When Edna was near the clearing in the last story, she couldn't see Tyrannosaurus. **Underline** 2 ways she knew that Tyrannosaurus was nearby.

    • She could taste it.   • She could feel its skin.
    • She could hear it.   • She could smell it.

6. What came into the clearing when Tyrannosaurus was moving

    back and forth? _____

7. At the beginning of today's story, Tyrannosaurus was fighting ▮▮▮.
    • Triceratops   • a mammoth   • a flying dinosaur

8. Who won the fight? _____

9. What kept making the earth rock from side to side?
    • earthquakes   • the volcano   • the storm

10. What made the boiling cloud of smoke? _____

11. Why did Edna fall down on the beach?

    _____

12. When the girls were in shallow water, what formed underwater?

    _____

13. Who fell into the crack? _____

14. What did the volcano do just after Edna got into the boat?

    _____

15. Did the girls know where they were going to go at the end of the

    story? _____

GO TO PART D IN YOUR TEXTBOOK.

A Story Items

1. What color was the water where it was shallow? _____

2. What color was the water where it was deepest? _____

3. Edna had blisters on her hands from _____.

4. As the girls sat in the lifeboat, they could see a billowing cloud in the distance. What was making that cloud?

   _____

5. Name 2 kinds of supplies you'd need to stay on the ocean for

   a long time. _____

6. In which direction were the girls drifting? _____

7. Edna was thirsty. Why didn't she drink some ocean water?
   - It was warm.
   - It was salty.
   - It was dirty.

8. What made the boat move faster and faster? _____

9. While the lifeboat was in the whirlpool, why did the clouds seem to be spinning?
   - because of the wind
   - because the boat was spinning
   - because she was sick

10. The water in the bottom of the boat was very warm, so that water had been in the boat for ▆▆▆.
    - a few seconds
    - a few minutes
    - a long time

11. Did the girls know how they got out of the whirlpool? _____

12. After Edna woke up, she saw fish. What color was the water?

_____

13. How deep is water that is green? _____

14. Why was Edna thinking about chewing on raw fish?

    • because she needed toothpaste

    • because she needed food

    • because she needed water

Review Item

15. Draw arrows at **X,** at **Y,** and at **Z** to show the way the melted rock moves.

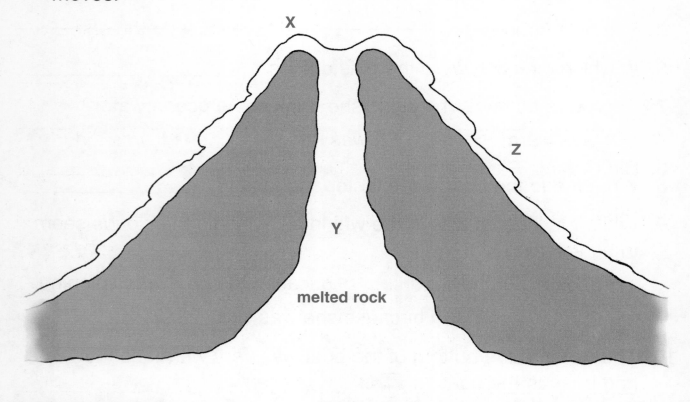

melted rock

GO TO PART C IN YOUR TEXTBOOK.

A **Story Items**

1. What did Edna see that told her a ship was in the distance?

   _____

2. How did she know it wasn't from the island?

   • It billowed.   • It didn't billow.   • It was black.

3. Whose ship was it? _____

4. Why did Edna feel ashamed when she saw her father?

   _____

5. The girls needed some care when they got back on the ship.

   Name 3 things they needed. _____

   _____

6. Did Captain Parker believe the girls' story? _____

7. What day of the week did the girls go overboard? _____

8. What day of the week did the girls think it was when they got

   back on the ship? _____

9. What day was it really when they got back on the ship?

   _____

10. What did Edna find to make her think the adventure really

    happened? _____

11. The sand in Edna's pocket must have come from

_____ .

Review Item

12. How long ago did dinosaurs live on Earth?

_____

13. What is it called when the earth shakes and cracks?

_____

14. Which letter shows a kangaroo? ____

15. Which letter shows a koala? ____

16. Which letter shows a platypus? ____

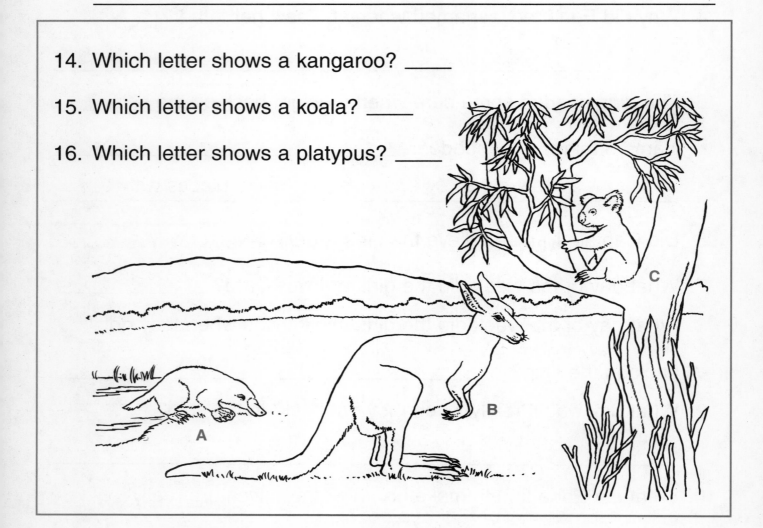

GO TO PART C IN YOUR TEXTBOOK.

A

1. Name 3 things that are made by humans. _____

    _____

2. What is a person doing when the person makes an object for the

    first time? _____

3. The person who makes an object for the first time is called an

    _____.

4. The object the person makes is called an _____.

B **Story Items**

5. **Underline** 2 reasons it was embarrassing to go places with
    Grandmother Esther.

    - She walked fast.   • She talked a lot.
    - She chewed gum.   • She mumbled to herself.
    - She talked loudly.

6. What did Grandmother Esther like to talk about?

    _____

7. Did she look at the displays of dinosaurs for a long time? _____

8. **Underline** 3 displays that Grandmother Esther wanted to see.

    - radios   • cave people   • clothing
    - airplanes   • horses   • automobiles

9. Grandmother Esther made a speech in the exhibit hall about the people who invented the airplane. How did Leonard feel?

_____

10. What did the other people in the exhibit hall do after the speech?

_____

Review Items

11. A mile is around _____ feet.

Here's how fast different things can go:

- 20 miles per hour
- 200 miles per hour
- 35 miles per hour
- 500 miles per hour

12. Which speed tells how fast a fast man can run?

_____

13. Which speed tells how fast a jet can fly?

_____

14. Which speed tells how fast a pointer can run?

_____

15. How many inches long is a yard? _____

16. About how many inches long is a meter? _____

GO TO PART D IN YOUR TEXTBOOK.

A Story Items

1. What was wrong with Grandmother Esther's water bed?

   _____

2. What did Grandmother Esther's folding bike sometimes do when

   a person was riding it? _____

3. **Underline** 2 things that Grandmother Esther ate for lunch.

   - apple
   - egg
   - donut
   - cake
   - cookie
   - sandwich

4. Did Leonard know what he wanted to invent? _____

5. At first Leonard thought that he couldn't be an inventor because

   _____

   _____.

6. Did Grandmother Esther agree? _____

7. The men who invented the first airplane saw a need. What

   need? _____

8. There was a need for the first automobile because people had
   problems with horses. **Underline** 2 problems.

   - Horses need care.
   - Horses are strong.
   - Horses are slow.
   - Horses like to run.

Review Items

9. A mile is around _____ feet.

Here's how fast different things can go:

- 500 miles per hour
- 35 miles per hour
- 200 miles per hour
- 20 miles per hour

10. Which speed tells how fast a pointer can run?

_____

11. Which speed tells how fast a jet can fly?

_____

12. Which speed tells how fast a fast man can run?

_____

13. If you go west from the United States, what ocean do you go

through? _____

14. What do we call the part of a ship where the cargo is carried?

_____

15. Some clocks have a hand that counts seconds. When that hand goes all the way around the clock, how much time has passed?

_____

16. The second hand on a clock went around 5 times. How much

time passed? _____

GO TO PART C IN YOUR TEXTBOOK.

A Story Items

1. What was wrong with the water bed that Grandmother Esther

   invented? _____

2. At first Leonard thought that he couldn't be an inventor because

   _____

   _____.

3. The first thing you do when you think like an inventor is find a

   _____.

4. What's the next thing you do?
   - Ask questions.
   - Meet the need.
   - Go to a museum.

5. Leonard's father had two ideas for inventions. One was
   something that cut down on traffic. What was his other idea?

   _____

6. Did Leonard's father think like an inventor? _____

7. Leonard's mother had an idea for an invention. What was it?

   _____

8. Had Grandmother Esther heard that idea before? _____

9. Did Grandmother Esther like that idea? _____

10. Did Leonard get any good ideas for inventions by talking to

people? _____

11. What did Leonard think the hardest part of being an inventor

was? _____

Review Items

12. Which letter shows a mammoth? _____

13. Which letter shows a saber-toothed tiger? _____

14. Which letter shows a horse from 40 thousand years ago? _____

F   G   H

GO TO PART C IN YOUR TEXTBOOK.

A Story Items

1. Leonard's mother had an idea for an invention. What was it?
   - a vacation that lasted all year long
   - an automatic grocery list writer
   - an automatic car washer

2. What did Leonard think the hardest part of being an inventor

   was? _____

3. Grandmother Esther told Leonard about 2 kinds of dreams.
   Underline those 2 kinds of dreams.
   - the dreams of a butterfly
   - the dreams of an inventor
   - silly wishes
   - day dreams

4. Why was Leonard ready to give up trying to be an inventor?

   _____

5. Leonard discovered that he needed a shoe checker. How did he

   know about that need? _____

   _____

6. Is asking people about their needs the best way to get ideas for

   inventions? _____

7. The best way to think like an inventor is to do things. When you

   do things, you look for _____
   that you have.

Review Items

8. You would have the most power if you pushed against one of

the handles. Which handle is that? ____

9. Which handle would give you the least amount of power? ____

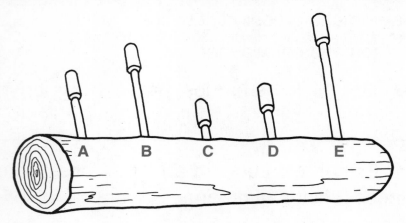

10. Which letter shows a kangaroo? ____

11. Which letter shows a koala? ____

12. Which letter shows a platypus? ____

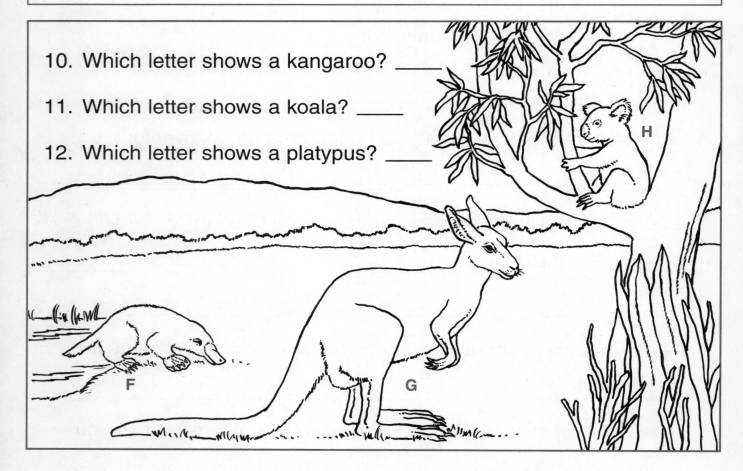

GO TO PART C IN YOUR TEXTBOOK.

A Story Items

1. When Leonard did things like washing the car, what did he pay

   attention to? _____

2. Each problem told Leonard about something he could

   _____ to solve the problem.

3. How long did Leonard try to find different problems?

   _____

4. What invention did he think would solve the problem he had with

   eggs? _____

5. What problem did Leonard have with his clothes at bedtime?

   _____

6. What invention did he think could solve that problem?

   _____

7. What invention did Leonard think could solve the problem he had

   when it rained? _____

8. What problem did Leonard have when he washed his dog?

   _____

9. Which invention did Leonard's mother think he should make?

   _____

10. Did Grandmother Esther name an invention that Leonard should

    make? _____

Review Items

Each statement tells about how far something goes or how fast something goes. Write **how far** or **how fast** for each item.

11. He ran 5 miles per hour. _____

12. He ran 5 miles. _____

13. The plane was 500 miles from New York City. _____

14. The plane was flying 500 miles per hour. _____

Use these names to answer the questions: **Tyrannosaurus, Triceratops.**

15. What is animal A? _____

16. What is animal B? _____

17. The first thing you do when you think like an inventor is find a

_____.

18. What's the next thing you do? _____

_____

GO TO PART C IN YOUR TEXTBOOK.

A Story Items

1. **Underline** the reasons that people on the street thought Grandmother Esther was mad at Leonard.

   - She made faces.
   - She pointed her finger.
   - She talked softly.
   - She talked loudly.
   - She kicked cats.

2. What invention did Leonard think could make his grandmother talk in a softer voice? _____

3. What would the invention do when Grandmother Esther talked louder? _____

Grandmother Esther explained how the electric eye works.

4. When somebody walks in the door, the body stops the beam of light from reaching the _____.

5. When the body stops the beam, what happens?

   _____

   _____

6. What does that tell the shopkeeper? _____

   _____

7. Why couldn't the people get into the bakery while Grandmother Esther talked? _____

   _____

8. What did those people say about Grandmother Esther's talk?

_____

9. How did Leonard feel? _____

10. Will the buzzer in the bakery make noise for picture A or

picture B? _____

11. What's the name of the invention shown in the pictures?

_____

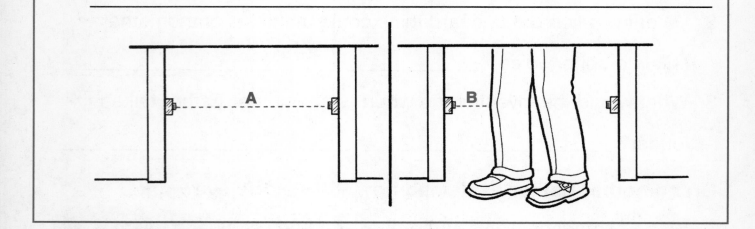

Review Items

12. How many inches long is a yard? _____

13. About how many inches long is a meter? _____

14. Which arrow shows the way the air will leave the jet engine? _____

15. Which arrow shows the way the jet will move? _____

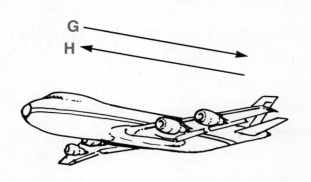

GO TO PART C IN YOUR TEXTBOOK.

A Story Items

1. Leonard got his idea for a great invention when Grandmother Esther told him to do something. What did she tell him to do?

_____

Leonard's original invention had problems.

2. What does the light in a dark room do when you walk into the

room? _____

3. What does the light do when you leave the room?

_____

4. Let's say two people walk into a dark room. What happens to the light in the room when the first person enters?

_____

5. What happens to the light when the second person enters?

_____

6. What will Leonard use to make the lights work automatically?

_____

7. Did Leonard's mother understand how his invention would work?

_____

8. Grandmother Esther told Leonard that every invention has

_____.

9. So what does the inventor have to do?

• quit   • solve the problem   • hide the problem

Here's the rule about an electric eye: **Each time the beam of light is broken, the light changes.** Shade the bulbs that are off for each problem. The first problem is already done for you.

10. The light is off. The beam is broken 4 times.

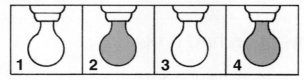

Is the light **on** or **off** at the end? _____

11. Here's another problem. The light is off. The beam is broken 8 times.
    a. Shade the bulbs that are off.

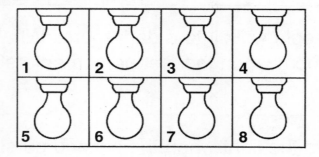

    b. Is the light **on** or **off** at the end? _____

12. Here's another problem. The light is off. The beam is broken 3 times.
    a. Shade the bulbs that are off.

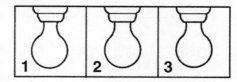

    b. Is the light **on** or **off** at the end? _____

GO TO PART C IN YOUR TEXTBOOK.

A Story Items

1. At the beginning of today's story, Leonard was trying to solve this problem: When a second person goes into the room, ▬▬.

   • the lights go on   • the lights stay on   • the lights go off

2. Leonard saw a sign that gave him a clue about solving his problem. What kind of sign did he see?

   _____

3. His invention had to know whether a person was moving ▬▬.

   • in or out   • fast or slow   • now or later

4. If a person moves **into** the room, which beam will be broken first—the **inside beam** or the **outside beam?**

   _____

5. Which beam will be broken next? _____

6. Will the lights turn **on** or **off?** _____

7. The picture shows two electric eye beams on the side of each door. The number **1** shows the beam that is broken first. The number **2** shows the beam that is broken next. On each picture, draw an arrow to show which way the person is moving. The first arrow is already drawn.

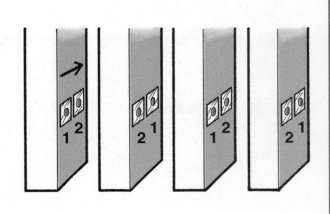

Here's the rule about an electric eye: **Each time the beam of light is broken, the light changes.**

8. a. The light is off. The beam is broken 3 times. Shade the bulbs that are off.

   b. Is the light **on** or **off** at the end? _____

9. a. The light is off. The beam is broken 6 times. Shade the bulbs that are off.

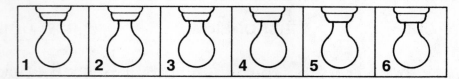

   b. Is the light **on** or **off** at the end? _____

10. a. The light is off. The beam is broken 5 times. Shade the bulbs that are off.

   b. Is the light **on** or **off** at the end? _____

GO TO PART C IN YOUR TEXTBOOK.

A Story Items

1. In the last story, Leonard saw a sign that gave him a clue about solving his problem. What kind of sign did he see?

_____

2. Would a person be moving into the room or out of the room if the

   inside beam is broken first? _____

3. Which way would a person be moving if the **outside** beam was

   broken first? _____

4. Leonard's original idea had a problem. What would happen if three people were in a room and one person left?

_____

5. Grandmother Esther told Leonard that his device could not

_____.

6. Letting water out of the sink gave Leonard an idea about his counter. What number did his counter have to count to?

_____

7. Every time somebody goes into the room, what does the counter do?

   • + 1   • − 1   • − 0

8. Every time somebody goes out of the room, what does the counter do?

   • + 1   • − 1   • − 0

9. What number does the counter end up at when the last person

leaves the room? _____

10. What happens to the lights when the counter is at zero?

_____

The solid arrows show people going into the room. The dotted arrows show people leaving the room. For each picture, **underline** the word that tells about the lights in the room.

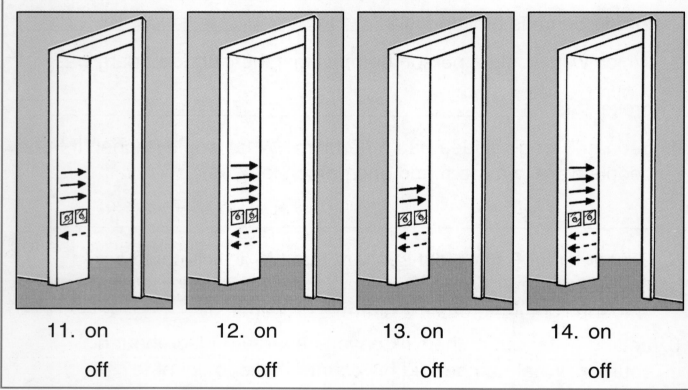

11. on

    off

12. on

    off

13. on

    off

14. on

    off

GO TO PART C IN YOUR TEXTBOOK.

A Story Items

1. What runs the electric eye?
   - city
   - electricity
   - grandmothers

2. What will run the counter? ____________________

3. Name 3 things Grandmother Esther does that are unusual for a grandmother. ____________________

   ____

4. Who paid for the electrical supplies? ____________________

5. How much did they cost? ____________________

6. The model was a little doorway that was about ______ tall.
   - 2 feet
   - 1 meter
   - 1 centimeter

7. There was a ____________________ connected to the top.

8. The light is off. A doll goes through the doorway. What happens to the light if the outside beam is broken first?

   ____

9. Did Leonard's device work? ____________________

10. Did he test it more than 1 time? ____________________

11. What does an inventor get to protect an invention?

    ____

12. If other people want to make copies of an invention, they have to make a deal with the ____________________.

13. What does the inventor usually make those people do?

_____

14. Special lawyers who get protection for inventions are called ▓▓▓.

 • patents   • doctors   • patent attorneys

15. How many meetings did Leonard and Grandmother Esther have

with a special lawyer? _____

16. How much money did Grandmother Esther pay the lawyer?

 • 3 thousand dollars   • 3 hundred dollars

 • 1 thousand dollars

Review Items

Use these names to answer the questions: **Tyrannosaurus, Triceratops.**

17. What is animal P? _____

18. What is animal J? _____

GO TO PART C IN YOUR TEXTBOOK.

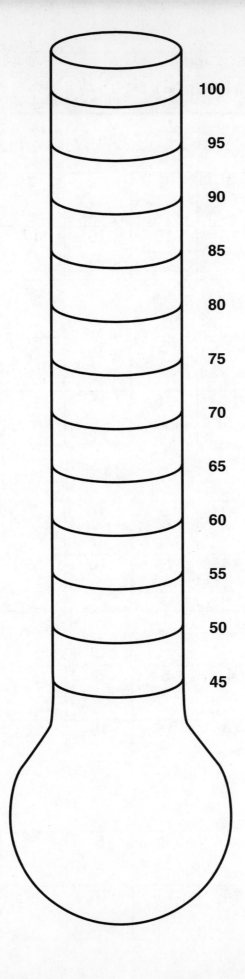

100

95

90

85

80

75

70

65

60

55

50

45

Fact Game Scorecards

Lesson 60

1	2	3	4	5	6	7	8	9	10
11	12	13	14	15	16	17	18	19	20

Lesson 70

1	2	3	4	5	6	7	8	9	10
11	12	13	14	15	16	17	18	19	20

Lesson 80

1	2	3	4	5	6	7	8	9	10
11	12	13	14	15	16	17	18	19	20

Lesson 90

1	2	3	4	5	6	7	8	9	10
11	12	13	14	15	16	17	18	19	20

Lesson 100

1	2	3	4	5	6	7	8	9	10
11	12	13	14	15	16	17	18	19	20